# DECODE　にほんご

Japanese Communication Made Easy

Keiko Tsujimura-Olsen

Cover:  Julien Thiebaud
Illustration:  Horahoop
Photo:  Juan Rodriguez

*AuthorHouse™*
*1663 Liberty Drive*
*Bloomington, IN 47403*
*www.authorhouse.com*
*Phone: 1-800-839-8640*



*First published by AuthorHouse 05/12/2011*

*ISBN: 978-1-4567-3749-8 (sc)*
*ISBN: 978-1-4567-3748-1 (e)*

*Library of Congress Control Number: 2011902927*

*Printed in the United States of America*



*This book is printed on acid-free paper.*

# Table of Contents

## Acknowledgements

This book became a reality because of many of my students, friends, and colleagues. Their input, advice, and contributions are truly appreciated.

I am very grateful to Mrs. Yasuko Nelson who inspired the idea in the first place.

Keiko Tsujimura-Olsen

# How to Use the Book

This book is written for a beginner of the Japanese language and serves as a communication guide book. It is small enough to carry around easily.

The book consists of places you may go and the possible communication that would take place. In each 'Let's Practice' area, you will find a series of sentences with boxes. By changing a word in a box you can create a brand new sentence.

For the audio portion of this book, please go to http://www.all4japanese.com/audiobookdownload.

hajimemashite
# はじめまして (How Do You Do?)

tanaka　ko n nichiwa
たなか：こんにちは。

suzuki　　　　　　　　　　　　　kochirawa
すずき：こんにちは。たなかさん、こちらは、

no　bura u n sa n desu
**NKT**の　ブラウンさんです。

hajimemashite　　　　　　　　de
ブラウン：はじめまして。**NKT**のブラウンで

su　do u zo　yoroshiku
す。どうぞ　よろしく。

たなか：はじめまして。たなかです。どうぞ

o nega i shimasu
よろしく　おねがいします。

Tanaka: Hello.
Suzuki: Hello. Mr. Tanaka, this is Mr. Brown of NKT.
Brown: How do you do? I'm Brown of NKT. Pleased to meet you.
Tanaka: How do you do. I'm Tanaka. Pleased to meet you.

ko n nichiwa
こんにちは........Hello. This greeting is used during the day. ( after around 10am to sun down.)

hajimemashite
はじめまして......How do you do? This is used when you meet a person for the first time.

do u zo yoroshiku
どうぞ　よろしく....It roughly means "I hope we have a good (long) relationship" and when used as a response to はじめまして it is usually translated "Pleased to meet you." どうぞ　よろしく can be used independently. If you add おねがいします (o nega i shimasu) it sounds politer.

tanaka
たなか...a surname

suzuki
すずき...a surname

bura u n
ブラウン...Brown

kochira
こちら...this (person)

wa・・・
__は … a particle. Subject marker. The letter は (ha) is pronounced "wa" when it functions as a particle.

no・・・
__の … the possessive particle. 's

sa n
さん…Mr., Mrs., Miss, Ms

desu
__です…to finish a sentence preceded by noun or adjective. Similar function with 'is, am, are.'

| | Affirmative | Negative |
|---|---|---|
| Present, future | desu<br>__です | dewa a rimase n<br>__ではありません<br>j a a rimase n<br>__じゃありません(less formal) |
| Past | deshita<br>__でした | dewa a rimase n de<br>__ではありませんで<br>shita<br>した<br>j a<br>__じゃありませんでした(less formal) |

__では（じゃ）ありません…negative form of
です.
ではありません is
more formal than
じゃありません

ka
__か…Makes a question.
NKT…a company name

Let's Practice

kaisha
かいしゃいん…a company employee

amerikajin　　　　　　mo
アメリカじん…an American　も….also

igirisujin
イギリスじん…a British

| suzuki<br>すずき<br>buraun<br>ブラウン<br>Your name | desu<br>です。 |
|---|---|

| NKT<br>Your company | の | すずき<br>Your name | です。 |
|---|---|---|---|

| watashi<br>（わたし）<br>ブラウンさん | は | kaishain<br>かいしゃいん<br>amerikajin<br>アメリカじん | です。 |
|---|---|---|---|

Questions:

| 1すずきさん<br>2ブラウンさん<br>kochira<br>3こちら | は | かいしゃいん<br>igirisujin<br>イギリスじん<br>donata<br>どなた | ですか。 |
|---|---|---|---|

Responses:

1 はい (ha i) すずきさん は

かいしゃいん です。

2 いいえ、(i i e) ブラウンさん は

イギリスじん では (じゃ) ありません。(dewa ja arimasen)

3 たなかさん です。(desu)

たなかさん は かいしゃいん です。

ブラウンさん も (mo) かいしゃいん です。

kuri にni n guyade
# クリーニングやで (At the Cleaners)

ten i n　i ras sh a i mase
てんいん：いらっしゃいませ。

kyaku　o　o nega i shimasu
きゃく：　クリーニングを　おねがいします

ha i　wa i sh atsuga　sanma i to
てんいん：はい、ワイシャツが　３まいと、

su　tsuga　ni ch akuto　zubo n ga
スーツが　２ちゃくと　ズボンが

i p p o n desune
１っぽんですね。

i tsu　dekimasuka
きゃく：　はい、いつ　できますか。

a sat t eno　yojini
てんいん：あさっての　４じに　できます。

i kuradesuka
きゃく：　いくらですか。

ze n bude　sanzengoju e n desu
てんいん：ぜんぶで　３０５０えんです。

j a　o nega i shimasu
きゃく：　じゃ、おねがいします。

Clerk: May I help you?
Customer: Yes, please.
Clerk: There are 3 shirts, 2 suits, and a pair of pants, right?
Customer: Yes, when are they ready?
Clerk: They'll be ready at 4o'clock the day after tomorrow.
Customer: How much?
Clerk: That will be 3050 yen altogether.
Customer: Okay.

kuri ni n guya
クリーニングや…dry cleaning shop

te n i n
てんいん….clerk

k y a ku
きゃく…customer

クリーニング…dry cleaning

i ras s h a i mase c
いらっしゃいませ…"Welcome, May I help you?" You will hear when you enter a store.

o nega i shimasu
おねがいします…..Please,

wa i s h a tsu
ワイシャツ…a shirt

su tsu
スーツ…a suit

zubo n
ズボン…pants

ha i
はい…Yes

i tsu
いつ…when

a sat t e
あさって…the day after tomorrow

ji
__じ…o'clock 4じ

ma i
__まい…a unit for counting paper-like objects

chaku
__ちゃく..a unit for counting suits

hon pon bon
__ほん（ぽん、ぼん）..a unit for counting long, stick-like objects

i kura zen bu
いくら…how much ぜんぶ…all

dekimasu
できます…finish,

かぞえかた（Counting system）

| Thin, paper-like objects | Stick-like objects |
|---|---|
| 1（いち）まい (i chi ma i) | 1（いっ）ぽん (i p pon) |
| 2（に）まい (ni ma i) | 2（に）ほん (hon) |
| 3（さん）まい (san) | 3（さん）ぼん (bon) |
| 4（よん）まい (yon) | 4（よん）ほん |
| 5（ご）まい (go) | 5（ご）ほん |
| 6（ろく）まい (roku) | 6（ろっ）ぽん (rop pon) |
| 7（なな）まい (nana) | 7（なな）ほん |
| 8（はち）まい (hachi) | 8（はっ）ぽん (hap pon) |
| 9（きゅう）まい (kyuu) | 9（きゅう）ほん |

j u u　　　　　　　j u p　po n
１０（じゅう）まい　　１０（じゅっ）ぽん

Suits, jackets, etc.

| | |
|---|---|
| i c　chaku<br>1（いっ）ちゃく | roku<br>6（ろく）ちゃく |
| ni<br>2（に）ちゃく | 7（なな）ちゃく |
| 3（さん）ちゃく | hac　chaku<br>8（はっ）ちゃく |
| 4（よん）ちゃく | 9（きゅう）ちゃく |
| 5（ご）ちゃく | j u c　chaku<br>１０（じゅっ）ちゃく |

じかん（Time）

| | |
|---|---|
| １：００ | i chi　ji<br>1（いち）じ |
| ２：００ | ni<br>2（に）じ |
| ３：００ | sa n<br>3（さん）じ |
| ４：００ | yo<br>4（よ）じ |
| ５：００ | 5（ご）じ |
| ６：００ | 6（ろく）じ |
| ７：００ | shichi<br>7（しち）じ |
| ８：００ | hachi<br>8（はち）じ |
| ９：００ | ku<br>9（く）じ |
| １０：００ | j u u<br>１０（じゅう）じ |
| １１：００ | j u u i chi<br>１１（じゅういち）じ |

| | | |
|---|---|---|
| １２：００ | juuni<br>１２（じゅうに）じ | |
| ９：００ | gozen<br>ごぜん９じ | 9am |
| ４：００ | gogo<br>ごご４じ | 4pm |

じかん

| | |
|---|---|
| ２：０５ | ni ji go fun<br>2（に）じ５（ご）ふん |
| １０ | jup pun<br>１０（じゅっ）ぷん |
| １５ | juugo fun<br>１５（じゅうご）ふん |
| ２０ | nijup pun<br>２０（にじゅっ）ぷん |
| ２５ | nijuugo fun<br>２５（にじゅうご）ふん |
| ３０ | sanjup pun<br>３０（さんじゅっ）ぷん、<br>han<br>はん |
| ３５ | sanjuugo fun<br>３５（さんじゅうご）ふん |
| ４０ | yonjup pun<br>４０（よんじゅっ）ぷん |
| ４５ | yonjuugo fun<br>４５（よんじゅうご）ふん |
| ５０ | gojup pun<br>５０（ごじゅっ）ぷん |
| ５５ | gojuugo fun<br>５５（ごじゅうご）ふん |

yo u bi
ようび

| | | | |
|---|---|---|---|
| getsuyo u bi<br>げつようび | Monday | o toto i<br>おととい | the day before yesterday |
| kayo u bi<br>かようび | Tuesday | kino u<br>きのう | yesterday |
| su i yo u bi<br>すいようび | Wednesday | k yo u<br>きょう | today |
| mokuyo u bi<br>もくようび | Thursday | a shita<br>あした | tomorrow |
| ki n yo u bi<br>きんようび | Friday | a sa t te<br>あさって | the day after tomorrow |
| doyo u bi<br>どようび | Saturday | | |
| nichiyo u bi<br>にちようび | Sunday | | |

Let's Practice

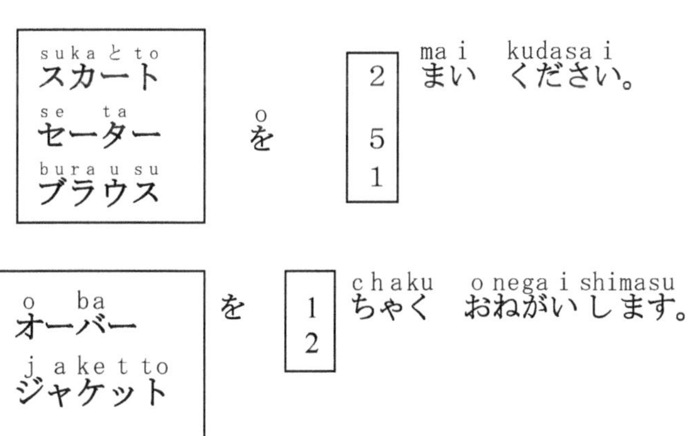

| | | | | |
|---|---|---|---|---|
| a shita<br>あした<br>su i yo u bi<br>すいようび<br>ki n<br>きんようび | no<br>の | ni ji<br>2じ<br>gojiha n<br>5じはん<br>goze n<br>ごぜん | ni<br>に | dekimasu<br>できます。 |

# be kari de
# ベーカリーで (At the Bakery)

ten in iras sha i mase
てんいん：いらっしゃいませ。

kyaku sorewa chokore topa n desuka
きゃく： それは チョコレートパンですか。

i i e korewa a n pa n desu
てんいん：いいえ、これは あんパンです。

i kuradesuka
きゃく： いくらですか。

hitotsu hyakugo e n desu
てんいん：ひとつ １０５えんです。

a rimasuka
きゃく： チョコレートパンは ありますか。

ha i a rega
てんいん：はい、あれが チョコレートパンです。

j a a kono mittsuto
きゃく： じゃあ、このあんパンを ３ つと

itsutsukudasa i
チョコレーパンを ５ つください。

てんいん：はい、あんパンが ３つと チョコレート

ne ze n bude s e n j u u
パンが ５つですね。ぜんぶで １０１０

e n desu
えんです。

Clerk: May I help you?
Customer: Is that Chocolate bun?
Clerk: No, this is bean-jam bun.
Customer: How much?
Clerk: One for 105 yen.
Customer: Is there (Do you have) a chocolate bun?
Clerk: Yes, that (over there) is a chocolate bun.
Customer: Well, give me 3 bean-jam buns and 5 chocolate buns.
Clerk: Yes, 3 bean-jam buns and 5 chocolate buns, right? It will be 1010 yen altogether.

be kari
ベーカリー…bakery ten in
てんいん…a store clerk

kyaku
きゃく………a customer

irasshaimase
いらっしゃいませ…May I help you? ( Welcome)

chokore topan
チョコレートパン…chocolate bun

anpan
あんパン…bean-jam bun

hitotsu
ひとつ…one en
えん…yen jaa
じゃあ…well, then

sore
それ…that (nearer to you than to me)

kore
これ…this (nearer to me than to you)

are
あれ…that over there

これ、それ、あれ can become subject by themselves.

kono
この＋N…this n (nearer to me than to you)

sono
その＋N…that n (nearer to you than to me)

ano
あの＋N…that N over there

この、その、あの requires noun to become a complete word

to　　　ze n bude
と…and　ぜんぶで…altogether

kudasa i　　　　i kura
ください…give me　いくら…how much

wa　ga
は、が…both Subject markers. が is used when the subject is emphasized.

a rimasuka
ありますか…Equivalence to "Is there…..?"

a rimasu
あります…existence of a(inanimate) thing. Similar to there is

ka
か… makes a question

| | Affirmative | Negative |
|---|---|---|
| Present/Future | a rimasu<br>あります | a rimase n<br>ありません |
| Past | a rimashita<br>ありました | a rimase n de<br>ありませんで<br>shita<br>した |

かず(Number)

１０　j u u
じゅう

１１　i chi
じゅういち

１２　ni
じゅうに

１３　sa n
じゅうさん

１４　shi　yo n
じゅうし（じゅうよん）

１５　go
じゅうご

roku
１６　じゅうろく

shichi　nana
１７　じゅうしち（じゅうなな）

hachi
１８　じゅうはち

kyuu　ku
１９　じゅうきゅう（じゅうく）

| | | | |
|---|---|---|---|
| ２０ | nijuu<br>にじゅう | ６０ | roku<br>ろくじゅう |
| ３０ | san<br>さんじゅう | ７０ | nana　shichi<br>ななじゅう（しちじゅう） |
| ４０ | yon<br>よんじゅう | ８０ | hachi<br>はちじゅう |
| ５０ | go<br>ごじゅう | ９０ | kyuu<br>きゅうじゅう |

| | | | |
|---|---|---|---|
| １００ | hyaku<br>ひゃく | ６００ | roppyaku<br>ろっぴゃく |
| ２００ | nihyaku<br>にひゃく | ７００ | ななひゃく |
| ３００ | byaku<br>さんびゃく | ８００ | happyaku<br>はっぴゃく |
| ４００ | よんひゃく | ９００ | きゅうひゃく |
| ５００ | ごひゃく | | |

| | | | |
|---|---|---|---|
| １０００ | sen<br>せん | ６０００ | ろくせん |
| ２０００ | にせん | ７０００ | ななせん |
| ３０００ | zen<br>さんぜん | ８０００ | hassen<br>はっせん |
| ４０００ | よんせん | ９０００ | きゅうせん |
| ５０００ | ごせん | | |

| | i chima n | | |
|---|---|---|---|
| １００００ | いちまん | ６００００ | ろくまん |
| ２００００ | にまん | ７００００ | ななまん |
| ３００００ | さんまん | ８００００ | はちまん |
| ４００００ | よんまん | ９００００ | きゅうまん |
| ５００００ | ごまん | １０００００ | じゅうまん |

Let's practice

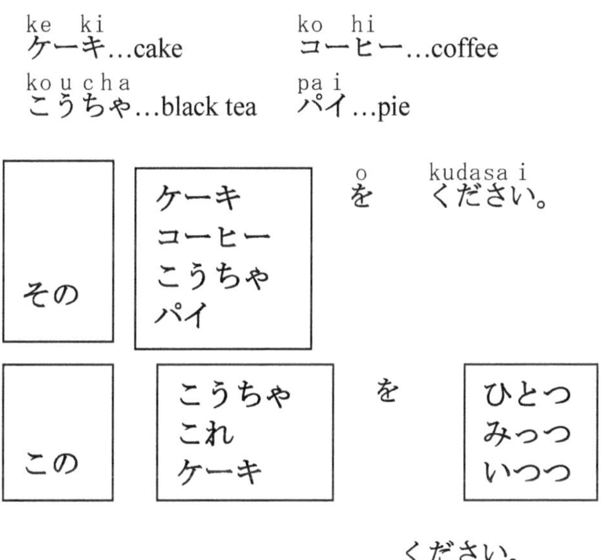


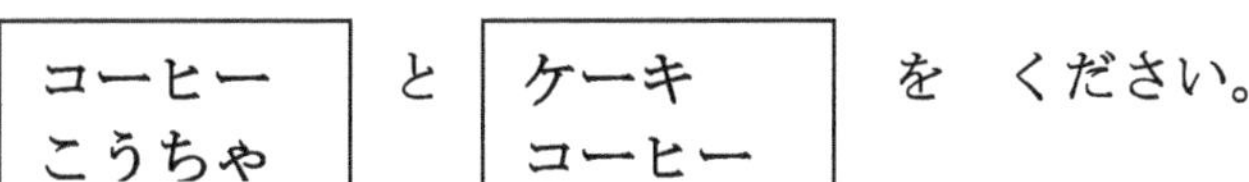

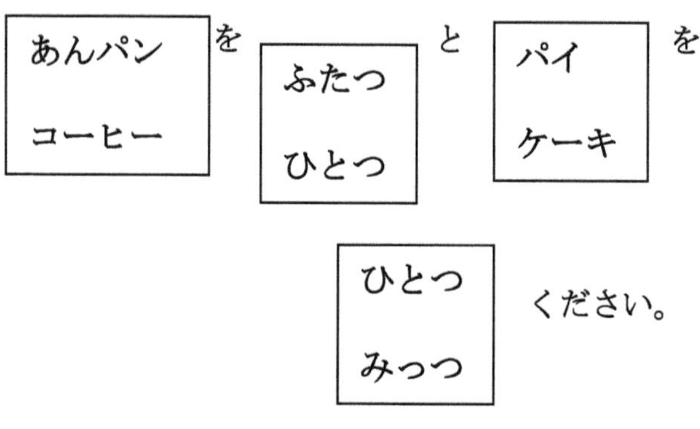


| | | |
|---|---|---|
| コーヒー<br>あんパン | が | ありますか。 |
| ケーキ<br>こうちゃ | は | ありません。 |

de n wa
# でんわ (Telephone)

bura u n　　　desu
ブラウン：　**NTK** のブラウンです。

kato u　　　sa n　　　suzuki
かとう：　ブラウン さん、かとうです。すずき

ni　re n rakushita i n desuga
さんに　れんらくしたいんですが、

sakino　　ba n go u wa
れんらくさきの　でんわばんごうは

na n ba n desuka
なんばんですか。

c h o t to　o machikudasa i
ブラウン：　ちょっと　おまちください。すずき
さんの　れんらくさきの　でんわ
ばんごうは、　０３－４３５６－
９８３４です。

a rigato u goza i mashita
かとう：　ありがとうございました。

Brown: Hello, this is Brown of NTK.
Kato: Mr. Brown, this is Kato. I want to contact with Mr. Suzuki. What is his contact number?
Brown: Just a minute please. Mr. Suzuki's contact number is 03-4356-9834.
Kato: Thank you.

re n raku
れんらく…contact

saki
れんらくさき…contact place

re n rakushimasu suru
れんらくします（れんらくする）…to contact. ( )is the dictionary form

shita i desu
V したいです… want to V

shita i n desuga
V したいんですが、….(I would) like to V,…….

| | Affirmative | Negative |
|---|---|---|
| Present/Future | ta i n<br>__たい（ん）<br>desu<br>です | takuna i<br>__たくない<br>n desu<br>（ん）です |
| Past | taka t ta<br>__たかった<br>n desu<br>（ん）です | takunaka t<br>__たくなかっ<br>ta n desu<br>た（ん）です |

o machikudasa i
おまちください…Please wait

machimasu　matsu
まちます（まつ）…to wait. ( ) is the dictionary form

| | Affirmative | Negative |
|---|---|---|
| Present／Future | まちます(wait)<br>れんらくします(contact) | まちません<br>れんらくしません |
| Past | まちました<br>れんらくしました | まちませんでした<br>れんらくしませんでした |

de n waba n go u
でんわばんごうtelephone number

でんわ…telephone　ばんごう…number

na n ba n
なんばん…what number

a rigato u goza i mashita
ありがとうございました…thank you

kazu
かず (Number)

| | | | |
|---|---|---|---|
| 1 | i chi<br>いち | 6 | roku<br>ろく |
| 2 | ni<br>に | 7 | nana　shichi<br>なな（しち） |
| 3 | sa n<br>さん | 8 | hachi<br>はち |
| 4 | yo n　shi<br>よん（し） | 9 | kyu u　ku<br>きゅう（く） |
| 5 | go<br>ご | １０ | j u u<br>じゅう |

Verbs

| | ta i<br>__たい | Affirmative | Negative |
|---|---|---|---|
| go | i kita<br>いきた<br>i<br>い | i kimasu<br>いきます | i kimase n<br>いきません |
| transfer (bus, train, etc.) | norika<br>のりか<br>e<br>えたい | のりかえます | のりかえません |
| get on | のりたい | のります | のりません |
| get off | o ri<br>おりたい | おります | おりません |
| wait | machi<br>まちたい | まちます | まちません |
| buy | ka i<br>かいたい | かいます | かいません |
| come | ki<br>きたい | きます | きません |
| read | yomi<br>よみたい | よみます | よみません |
| eat | tabe<br>たべたい | たべます | たべません |
| drink | nomi<br>のみたい | のみます | のみません |
| get up | o ki<br>おきたい | おきます | おきません |

| | | | |
|---|---|---|---|
| sleep | ne<br>ねたい | ねます | ねません |
| tell, teach | o shi<br>おし<br>e<br>えたい | おしえます | おしえません |
| listen | kiki<br>ききたい | ききます | ききません |

Let's practice.

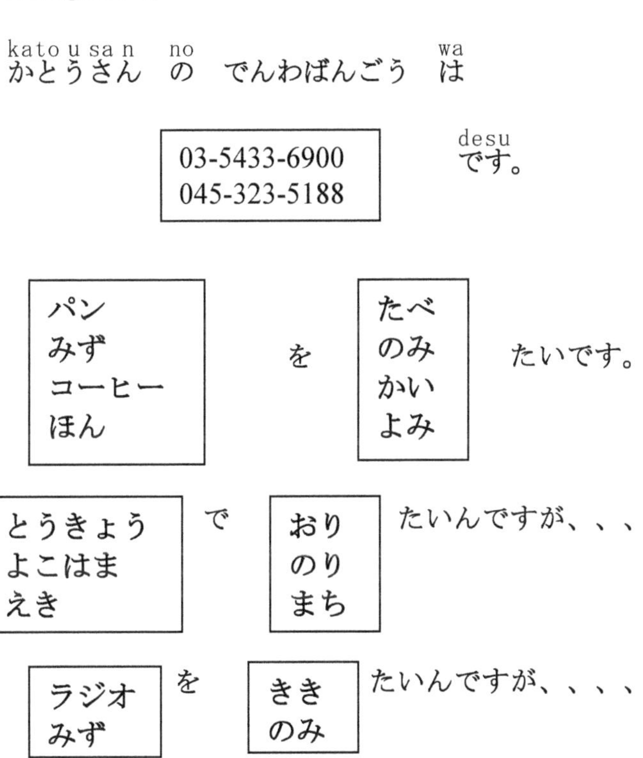

kato u sa n　no　　　　　　wa
かとうさん　の　でんわばんごう　は

03-5433-6900
045-323-5188

desu
です。

パン
みず
コーヒー
ほん
を
たべ
のみ
かい
よみ
たいです。

とうきょう
よこはま
えき
で
おり
のり
まち
たいんですが、、、

ラジオ
みず
を
きき
のみ
たいんですが、、、、

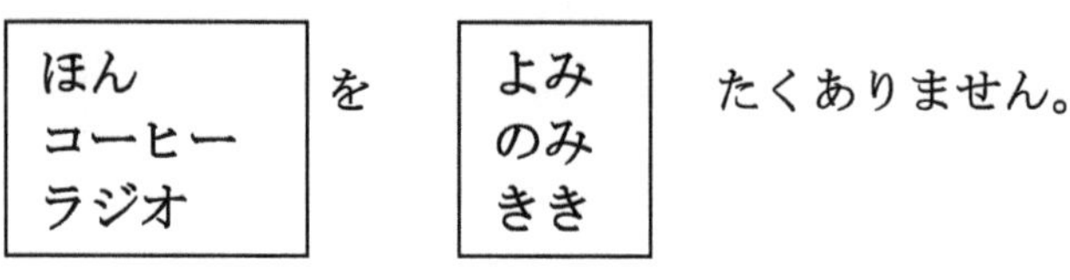


| バス<br>しながわ | に | のり<br>いき | たくないのですが、、、 |
|---|---|---|---|

## den shade
## でんしゃで (In the Train)

shashouno　　konodenshawa　touekide
しゃしょうの：　このでんしゃは　とうえきで

anaunsu　　sharyouno　kirihanashio
アナウンス　　しゃりょうの　きりはなしを

shimasu　　ushironoyon
します。、、うしろの４

ryouwa　hanedaikini
りょうは　はねだいきに

narimasu　onorimachigaeno
なります。おのりまちがえの

naiyouni　onegaishimasu
ないように　おねがいします。

sumisu　　sumimasen　shinagawani
スミス：　　すみません、しながわに

ikitaindesuga
いきたいんですが　この

sharyouwa
しゃりょうは　しながわに

ikimasuka
いきますか。

tonarino　hito　　iie　wa
となりの　ひと：　いいえ、このしゃりょうは

hanedaikidesu　maeno
はねだいきです。まえの

ni　norikaete
しゃりょうに　のりかえて

kudasai
ください。

doumo　arigatou
スミス：　　どうも、ありがとう

| | |
|---|---|
| A conductor's: announcement | This train will be detached at this station. … The last 4 cars will be for Haneda. Please make sure you are in the right car. |
| Smith: | Excuse me, I want to go to Shinagawa, does this car go to Shinagawa? |
| The person : next to Mr. Smith | No, this goes to Haneda. You need to the car in front. |
| Smith: | Thank you. |

de n sha　　　　 s h a s h o u
でんしゃ…train　しゃしょう…a conductor

a na u n su　　　　　　　　　sumisu
アナウンス…announcement　スミス… Smith

tonarino　hito
となりの　ひと…the person next to you

となり…next　ひと…person

to u e ki　　　　　　s h a r y o u
とうえき…this station　しゃりょう… (train) cars

kirihanashi
きりはなし… detach

r y o u
りょう…　the counter for train cars

u shiro　　　　　　ma e
うしろ… the back　まえ… the front

o norimachiga
(お)のりまちがい…getting on the wrong car

norimasu　noru
のります（のる）…to get on ( )　is the dictionary form

machiga i
まちがい…mistake

na i yo u ni
ないように…so, there is no…

shinagawa
しながわ,,,Shinagawa(name of place)

haneda i ki
はねだいき…For Haneda

i kita i n desuga t
いきたいんですが….want to go

ta i n desu ga
__たい（ん）です（が） want to (do V)

norika e masu
のりかえます…change a train, (plain, bus, etc.)

te kudasa i
のりかえて　ください…please change a train, etc.

Verbs

| | te<br>__て | Affirmative | Negative |
|---|---|---|---|
| go | i t te<br>いって | i kimasu<br>いきます | i kimase n<br>いきません |
| transfer | norika<br>のりか<br>e te<br>えて | norika e ma<br>のりかえま<br>su<br>す | norika e ma<br>のりかえま<br>se n<br>せん |
| get on | no t te<br>のって | norimasu<br>のります | norimase n<br>のりません |
| get off | o rite<br>おりて | o rimasu<br>おります | o rimase n<br>おりません |
| wait | ma t te<br>まって | machimasu<br>まちます | machimase n<br>まちません |
| buy | ka t te<br>かって | ka i masu<br>かいます | ka i mase n<br>かいません |
| come | kite<br>きて | kimasu<br>きます | kimase n<br>きません |
| read | yo n de<br>よんで | yomimasu<br>よみます | yomimase n<br>よみません |
| eat | tabete<br>たべて | tabemasu<br>たべます | tabemase n<br>たべません |
| drink | no n de<br>のんで | nomimasu<br>のみます | nomimase n<br>のみません |

| get up | o kite<br>おきて | o kimasu<br>おきます | o kimase n<br>おきません |
|---|---|---|---|
| sleep | nete<br>ねて | nemasu<br>ねます | nemase n<br>ねません |
| tell, teach | o shi<br>おし<br>e te<br>えて | o shi e masu<br>おしえます | o shi e mase<br>おしえませ<br>n<br>ん |
| listen | ki i te<br>きいて | kikimasu<br>ききます | kikimase n<br>ききません |

Let's practice.

まっ
おき
おしえ

tekudasa i
てください。

しながわ
はねだ
よこはま

ni
に

i kita i n desuga
いきたいんですが、、、

しぶや
よこはま
しながわ

で

おり
のりかえ
のっ

てください。

## de n s h a no e k i de
## でんしゃのえきで (At the Train Station)

k y a ku　　　　o o sakamadeno　o u fukuki p pu o
きゃく：　おおさかまでの　おうふくきっぷを

m a i　o n e g a i shimasu
１まい　おねがいします。

e ki i n　　jiyu u sekidesuka　soretomo　shite
えきいん：　じゆうせきですか、それとも　して

i sekidesuka
いせきですか。

i ma　ko n de i masuka
きゃく：　いま、こんでいますか。

e e
えきいん：　ええ。

j a
きゃく：　じゃ、していせきで　おねがいしま

i kuradesuka
す。いくらですか。

niman　happyaku e n desu
えきいん：　２０，８００えんです。

na n ba n se n desuka
きゃく：　なんばんせんですか。

えきいん：　８ばんせんです。

do u mo
きゃく：　どうも。

Translation

Customer: One round trip ticket to Oosaka, please.
Station staff:: Non reserved seat or reserved seat?
Customer: Is it crowded now?
Station staff: Yes, I'm afraid so.
Customer: Well, I'll take reserved seat. How much?
Station staff: 20,800.
Customer: Which track?
Station staff: Track number 8.
Customer: Thank you.

de n s h a e ki
でんしゃ….a train えき…a .train station

e ki i n k y a ku
えきいん…a station staff きゃく…customer

no・・・ soretomo
の … .a possessive particle "of" それとも…or

o o saka
おおさか….name of the city

o u fukuki p pu
おうふくきっぷ…a round trip ticket

katamichi
かたみちきっぷ…a one-way ticket

jiyu u seki
じゆうせき……non reserved seat

shite i
していせき……..reserved seat

ko n de i masuka
こんでいますか…..is it crowded?

komimasu komu
こみます（こむ）…crowded

sukimasu suku
すきます（すく）..not crowded

na n ba n se n
なんばんせん…which track( number)

ho mu
__ばんせん …..＃track ホーム…platform

yamanotese n
やまのてせん…Yamanote Line

chiyoda
ちよだせん……Chiyoda Line

michi
みち ….road

Verbs

| | Progressive<br>te i ma<br>—ていま<br>su<br>す | Neg. Progressive<br>te i mase<br>—ていませ<br>n<br>ん | Affirm.<br>masu<br>—ます | Neg.<br>mase<br>ませ<br>n<br>ん. |
|---|---|---|---|---|
| crowded | こんでいます | こんでいません | こみます | こみません |
| empty | すいています | すいていません | すきます | すきません |

Let's Practice

| よこはま<br>しながわ | までの | かたみちきっぷ<br>おうふくきっぷ | を |
|---|---|---|---|

| 2まい<br>5まい | おねがいします。 |
|---|---|

| やまのてせん | の | ホーム<br>していせき<br>5ばんせん<br>ちよだせん | は　どこですか。 |
|---|---|---|---|

| でんしゃ<br>みち | は | こんで<br>すいて | います。 |
|---|---|---|---|

# o i s h a s a n de
# おいしゃさんで (Doctor's Office)

| | |
|---|---|
| i s h a<br>いしゃ： | do u shimashitaka<br>どうしましたか。 |
| sumisu<br>スミス： | nodoga kayukute kuchibiruga<br>のどが かゆくて、くちびるが<br>harete i masu<br>はれています。 |
| いしゃ： | nani o tabemashitaka<br>なにを たべましたか。 |
| スミス： | sashimi o<br>さしみを たべました。 |
| いしゃ： | ka i<br>かいを たべましたか。 |
| スミス： | ha i<br>はい。 |
| いしゃ： | s h okumotsu a rerugi desu<br>しょくもつアレルギーです。<br>kusuri o a gemash o u<br>くすりを あげましょう。<br>yak k y o kude kat t ekudasa i<br>やっきょくで かってください。 |

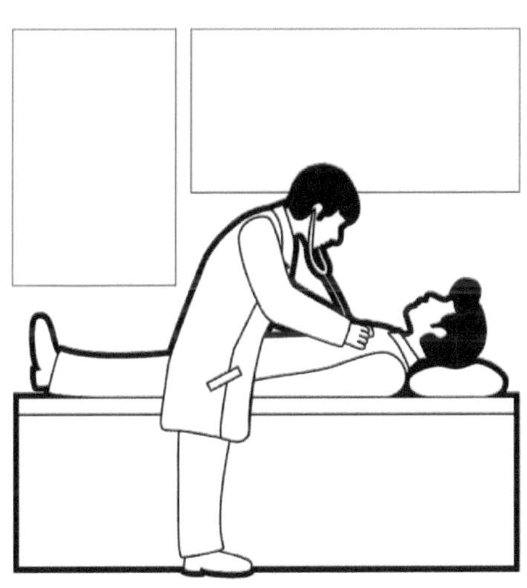

Doctor: What seems to be the problem?
Smith: My throat is itchy and my lips are swollen.
Doctor: What did you eat?
Smith: I ate sashimi.
Doctor: Did you eat shell fish?
Smith: Yes, I did.
Doctor: You have the food allergy. I will write you a prescription. Please go to a pharmacy and get it.

nodo kayu i kuchibiru
のど,,,throat かゆい…itchy くちびる…lips

harete i masu hareru
はれています（はれる）…swollen

nani shokumotsu a rerugi
なに…what しょくもつアレルギー…food allergy

tabemashita taberu
たべました（たべる）…ate (eat)

sashimi a ka i
さしみ…Sashimi(law fish) かい…shell fish

kusuri
くすり…medicine

a gemashou
あげましょう(I will) give you

a gemasu a geru
あげます（あげる）(I) give

yakkyoku kusuriya
やっきょく（くすりや）…a drug store, a pharmacy

kattekudasai
かってください…please buy

ka i masu ka u
かいます（かう）…buy

i ta i desu i ta i
いたいです（いたい）…have a pain

shimasu suru
します（する）…(I) have, do

shite i masu
しています…(I) am having, is (are) doing

a rimasu　a ru
ありますます（ある）…(I) have, there is

kakarimasu　kakaru
かかります（かかる）…have,

a tama　mimi　ha　me
あたま…head　みみ…ear　は…tooth　め…eye

o naka　koko
おなか…stomach　ここ…here

samuke　zutsu u
さむけ…chills　ずつう…headache

hakike
はきけ… nauseous

geri　be n pi
げり…diarrhea　べんぴ…constipation

to u nyo u byo u
とうにょうびょう…diabetes

ze n soku　kika n shi e n
ぜんそく…asthma　きかん しえん…bronchitis

r yu u ka n
りゅうかん…flu

ni s sha byo u
にっしゃびょう…sunstroke

s h okuc h u u doku
しょくちゅうどく…food poisoning

kaze o　hi i te i masu　hiku
かぜを　ひいています（ひく）have a cold

mema i ga　shimasu ….
めまいが　します ….feel dizzy

Let's Practice

I have headache, sore throat, earache, etc.

| |
|---|
| あたま<br>のど<br>みみ<br>おなか<br>は<br>ここ |

ga　i ta i desu
が　いたいです。

It always, sometimes, etc. hurts.

| |
|---|
| いつも<br>ときどき」 |

i ta i desu
いたいです

I have chills, feel nauseous, etc.

| |
|---|
| さむけ<br>はきけ |

ga　shimasu
が　します。

I have had diarrhea, constipations, etc.

| |
|---|
| げり<br>べんぴ |

o　shite i masu
を　しています。

I've had a cold.

kaze o hi i te i masu
かぜ を ひいています。

I have allergies, asthma, etc.

| アレルギー<br>ぜんそく<br>とうにょうびょう | ga a rimasu<br>が ありますす。 |
|---|---|

## kusuriyade
## くすりやで (At the Pharmacy)

| | |
|---|---|
| tenin<br>てんいん： | irasshaimase nanio osaga<br>いらっしゃいませ。なにを おさが |
| | shidesuka<br>しですか。 |
| sumisu<br>スミス： | zutsuuno kusuriga arimasuka<br>ずつうの くすりが ありますか。 |
| てんいん： | hai<br>はい。 |
| スミス： | dorega yoku kikimasuka<br>どれが よく ききますか。 |
| てんいん： | korega iidesuyo<br>これが いいですよ。 |
| スミス： | ja soreo kudasai<br>じゃ、 それを ください。 |

Store clerk: May I help you?
Smith: Do you have a medicine for headache?
Store clerk: Yes.
Smith: Which one works best?
Store clerk: I think this one is good.
Smith: Okay, I will take that one.

kusuriya　　　　　　　　　　　　　　　nani
くすりや…a drug store (pharmacy)　なに…what

o sagashidesuka
おさがしですか…(Are you looking for?)

sagashimasu　sagasu
さがします（さがす）…look for, seek

zutsu u　　　　　kusuri
ずつう…headache　くすり…medicine

yoku　　i i
よく…well　いい…good

dore　　i
どれ…which　い…stomach

kikimasu　kiku
ききます（きく）… work, effective

kazegusuri　　　　　　　nodo
かぜぐすり,,,cold medicine　のど…throat

megusuri
めぐすり…eye drop

a mari　　　mase n
あまり　Verb+ません…not so V

Let's practice

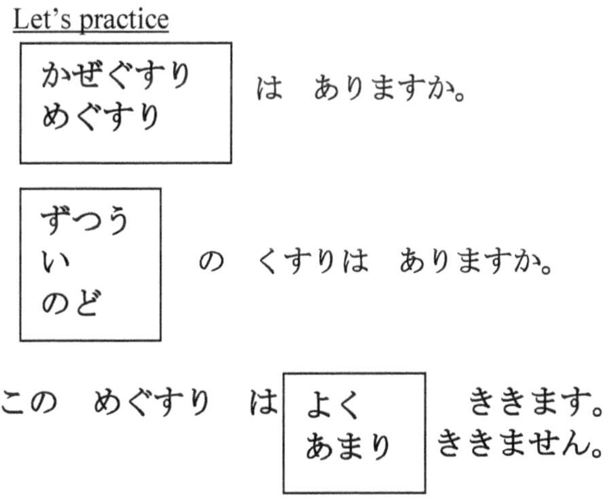

## gi n ko u de
## ぎんこうで (At the Bank)

sumisu　　　　　sumimase n
スミス：　　　　すみません。

gi n ko u i n　　　ha i　sokono　ba n go u fuda o
ぎんこういん：　はい、そこの　ばんごうふだを

to t te　o machikudasa i
とって　おまちください。

＊＊＊＊＊＊＊＊＊＊＊＊＊＊＊＊＊＊＊＊＊

ba n no　kata
ぎんこういん：　６７ばんの　かた。

r y o u ga e o
スミス：　　　　はい、　りょうがえを

o nega i shimasu
おねがいします。

a merikadorukara　nihp
ぎんこういん：　はい、アメリカドルから　にほ

n e n desune　s h o u s h o u
んえんですね。しょうしょう

o machikudasa i
おまちください。

＊　＊＊＊＊＊＊＊＊＊＊＊＊＊＊＊＊＊＊＊

sama　ba n no　madogu
ぎんこういん：　スミスさま。２ばんの　まどぐ

chini　o i dekudasa i
ちに　おいでください。

スミス：　　　　はい。

o matase i tashimashita　ho n ji
ぎんこういん：　おまたせいたしました。ほんじ

tsuno　re　towa　doru
つの　レートは　1ドル　１１

5

e n desunode　e n
えんですので　１００５０えん

ni　narimasu
に　なります。

Smith: Excuse me.
Bank clerk: Please take that number card and wait.
**********************************

Bank clerk: Number 67.
Smith: Yes, I need to exchange money.
Bank clerk: Yes, to change from US dollar to Japanese yen, right? Please wait at the seat.

---

Bank clerk: Mr. Smith, please come to the window #2.
Smith: Yes.
Bank clerk: Thank you for waiting. Today's rate is 115 yen for a dollar. It will be 10050 yen.

ba n go u fuda
ばんごうふだ…number card

to t te torimasu
とって（とります）…take

o machikudasa i kata
おまちください…please wait かた…person

r y o u ga e
りょうがえ…exchange

a merikadoru niho n e n
アメリカドル…US dollar にほんえん..Japanese yen

s h o u s h o u niba n
しょうしょう…a little ２ばん…number 2

madoguchi o i dekudasa i
まどぐち…window おいでください…please come

o mataseshimashita
おまたせしました…thank you for waiting

ho n jitsu re to node
ほんじつ…today レート…rate ので…because

narimasu naru
なります（なる）…become

More words
はし…chopsticks しょるい…official paper

ホーム…plat form
しぶや….Shibuya (a name of place)

つかって（つかう）…use
たべて（たべる）….eat
もって（もつ）…..take　　きて（くる）….come
いって（いく）….go
でんわして（でんわする）….phone
にちようび….Sunday　やすみ….holiday, break
ブランドもの….brand goods　たかい….expensive
テニス…tennis
あめ …rain　ちゅうし…cancel
かいます（かう）…buy
おいしくない…doesn't taste good
ケーキ…cake　やすい…cheap
しんぶん…newspaper
おもしろい….interesting　よみます（よむ）…read

Let's practice

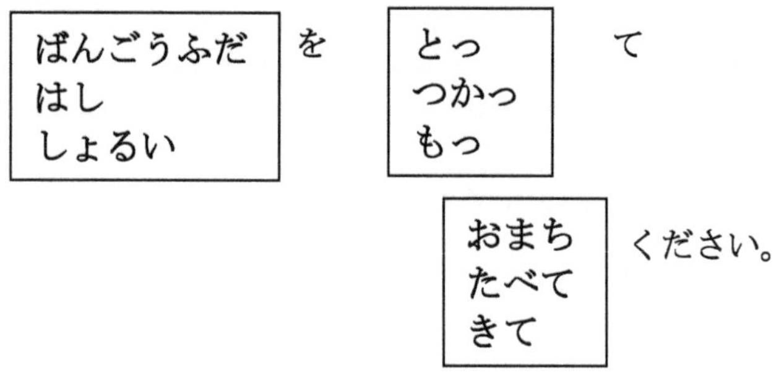

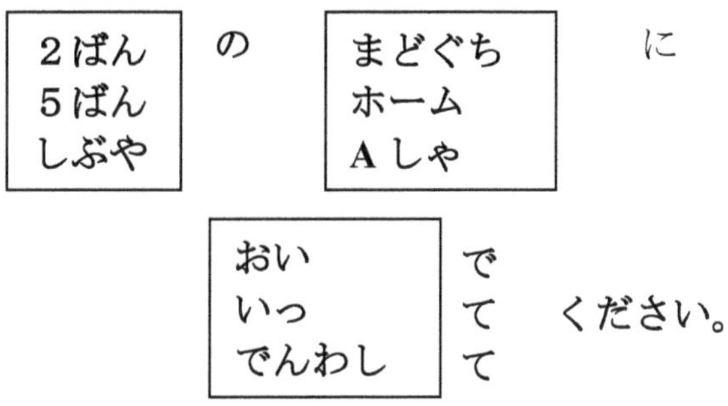


The following expressions are more colloquial than
「……ですので、____。」

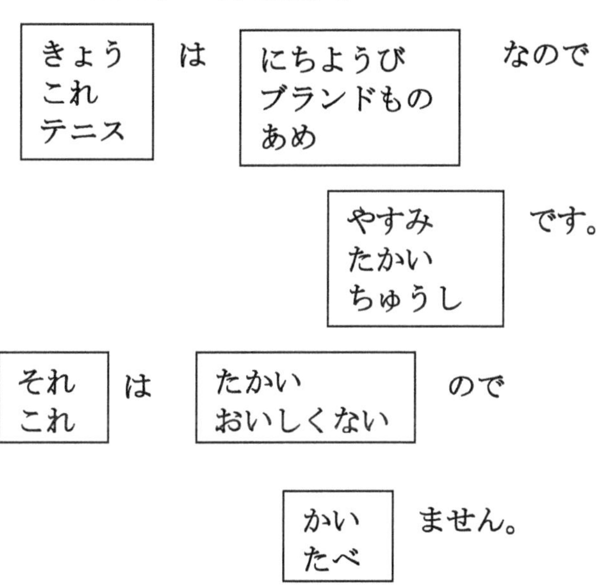

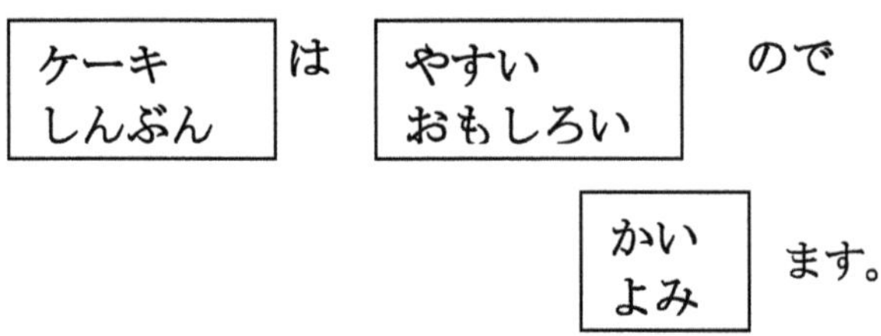
ケーキ
しんぶん
は
やすい
おもしろい
ので
かい
よみ
ます。

yuubinkyokude
# ゆうびんきょくで (At the Post Office)

sumisu　　kore o　amerikani　okuritai n
スミス：　これを　アメリカに　おくりたいん

desuga
ですが、、

kyokuin　nande　okurimasuka
きょくいん：なんで　おくりますか。

koukuubinto　sarubinwa
スミス：　こうくうびんと　ＳＡＬびんは

dou　chigaimasuka
どう　ちがいますか。

wa　yaku　isshu　u
きよくいん：こうくうびんは　やく　１しゅう

kande　tsukimasuは
かんで　つきます。　ＳＡＬびんは

nishuukan　guraide
２しゅうかん　ぐらいで　つきます。

to　dewa　dochira
スミス：　こうくうびんと　**SAL**では、どちら

nohouga　yasuidesuka
のほうが　やすいですか。

ende
きょくいん：こうくうびんは　１５０００えんで、
ＳＡＬは　９０００えんです。

ja　onegaishimasu
スミス：　じゃ、ＳＡＬで　おねがいします。

Smith: I would like to send this to the US.
Mail clerk: How would you like to send?
Smith: What is the difference between air mail and SAL?
Mail clerk: Air mail takes about a week and SAL takes about 10days.
Smith: How much?
Mail clerk: Air mail is 15000 yen and SAL is 9000 yen.
Smith: Well, please send it by SAL.

yu u bi n k y o ku
ゆうびんきょく …post office

o kurita i n desuga
おくりたいんですが …I would like to send,,,

o kurita i desu
おくりたいです I would like to send

o kurimasu o kuru
おくります（おくる）send

ko u ku u bi n
こうくうびん…air mail (takes about one week)

s aru
SAL …economy air(faster than surface mail and cheaper than air mail, takes 10-14 days) (Surface Air Lifted mail)

EMS…express air service (takes 3-4days.)

funabi n
ふなびん…surface mail (takes about a month)

s hu u ka n
１しゅうかん…one week しゅうかん… for week

gura i tsukimasu tsuku
ぐらい…about つきます（つく）…arrive

dochira ho u
どちら…which ほう…way

yasu i taka i
やすい…cheap たかい…expensive

haya i o so i yori
はやい…fast おそい…slow より…than

Let's practice.

| SAL びん | | noho u ga<br>のほうが | |
|---|---|---|---|
| こうくうびん | yori<br>より | やすい<br>おそい | です。 |

| ふなびん | は | SAL びん | より |
|---|---|---|---|
| | | やすい<br>おそい | です。 |

| EMS | は | こうくうびん | より |
|---|---|---|---|
| | | はやい<br>たかい | です。 |

## houmon
## ほうもん (Visiting Someone)

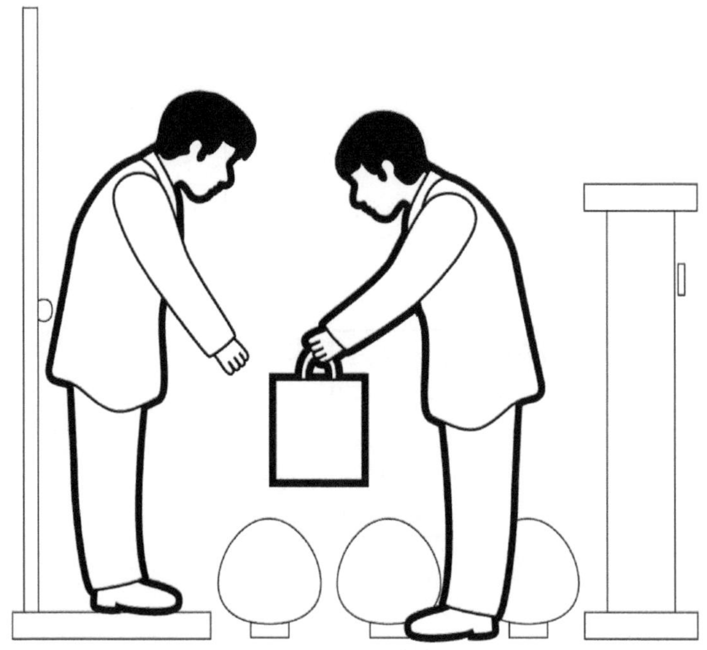

sumisu　kon nichiwa
スミス：こんにちは。

suzuki　yoku　irasshaimashita　douzo
すずき：よく　いらっしゃいました。どうぞ。

　　　　ojamashimasu　kore　sukoshidesuga
スミス：おじゃまします。これ　すこしですが、
　　　　**(present a small gift)**

　　　　doumo　sumimasen　douzo　kochi
すずき：どうも　すみません。どうぞ　こち
　　　　rae
　　　　らへ。

スミス：どうも。

o i shiso u desune korewa na n desuka
スミス：おいしそうですね。これは　なんですか。

o sushidesu
すずき：おすしです。

totemo kire i desune
すみす：とても　きれいですね。

do u zo meshi a ga t tekudasa i
すずき：どうぞ　めしあがってください。

i tadakimasu totemo o i shi i desu
スミス：いただきます。とても　おいしいです。

mo u sukoshi i kagadesuka
すずき：もう　すこし　いかがですか。

mo u o nakaga i p pa i desu
スミス：もう　おなかが　いっぱいです。

gochiso u samadeshita
ごちそうさまでした。

Smith: Good afternoon.
Suzuki: I'm glad you made it. Please come in.
Smith: Thank you. This is something small…(giving your gift)
Suzuki: Thank you. Please come this way.

---

Smith: It looks delicious. What is this?
Suzuki: It is Japanese sushi.
Smith: It looks so pretty.
Suzuki: Please have some.
Smith: Thank you. It is very tasty.
Suzuki: Would you like some more?
Smith: No, thank you. I am full. It was very good.

yoku
よく…well

i ra s sha i mashita
いらっしゃいました…came (politer than きました)

o j a mashimasu
おじゃまします…an expression when you enter someone's house, room, etc. means "excuse my intrusion"

sukoshi
すこし…a little, small

kochira e
こちらへ…this way

o i shiso u desu
おいしそうです…looks delicious

o i shi i desu
おいしいです….delicious

ne
、、、ね...____, isn't it?

o sushi sushi
おすし（すし）….sushi

totemo
とても…very

kire i
きれい….pretty, beautiful

meshi a ga t tekudasa i
めしあがってください….please eat

i tadakimasu
いただきます...an expression when you are about to eat a meal ( polite way to say " I'm going to eat)

mo u
もう…already

o naka
おなか…stomach

i p pa i
いっぱい…full

gochiso u sama
ごちそうさま….an expression when you finish the meal (means " it was a feast")

More words

taka i　　　　　　takaso u
たかい…expensive　たかそう…looks expensive

yasu i　　　　yasuso u
やすい…cheap　やすそう…looks cheap

o o ki i　　　　o o kiso u
おおきい…big, large　おおきそう…looks big, large

chi i sa i　　　chi i saso u
ちいさい…small　ちいさそう…looks small

Let's Practice.

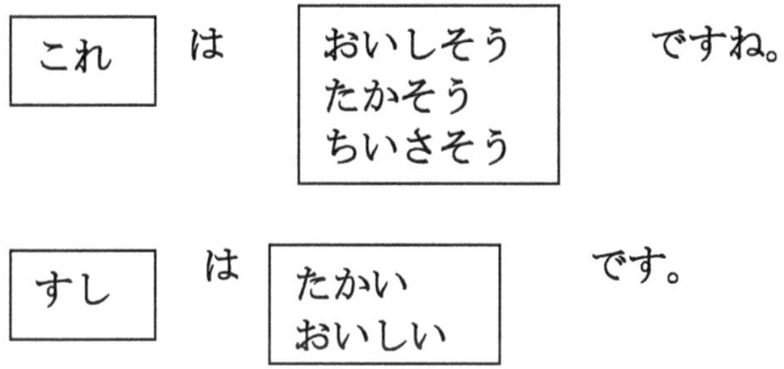

# takushi de
# タクシーで (In the Taxi)

unten shu dochiramadedesuka
うんてんしゅ： どちらまでですか。

sumisu yokohama e kimade o negai
スミス： よこはまえきまで おねがい

shimasu
します。

higashiguchidesuka soretomo
うんてんしゅ： ひがしぐちですか、それとも

nishiguchidesuka
にしぐちですか。

made
スミス： にしぐちまで おねがいします。

o machido u sama
うんてんしゅ： おまちどうさま。

i kuradesuka
スミス： いくらですか。

e n desu
うんてんしゅ： ４０９０えんです。

korede
スミス： これで おねがいします。

reshi to o
レシートを おねがいします。

ha i e n no o tsuridesu
うんてんしゅ： はい。１０えんの おつりです。

do u mo
スミス： どうも。

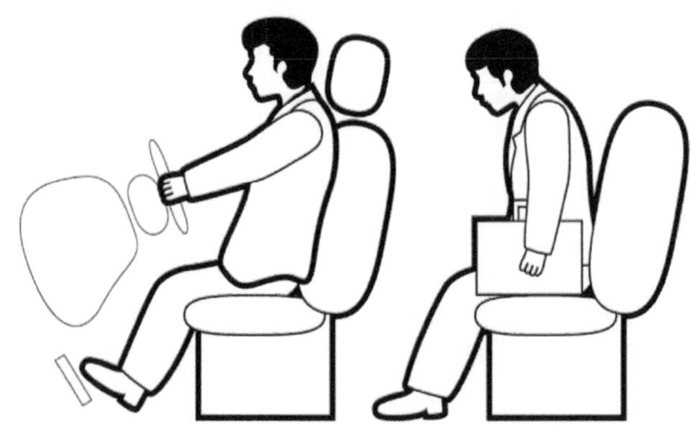

Driver: Where to:
Smith: Yokohama Station, please.
Driver: Do you want East or West entrance?
Smith: West, please.
Driver: Here we are.
Smith: How much?
Driver: 4090 yen.
Smith: Here you go. I need the receipt, too.
Driver: Sure and here is your change.
Smith: Thank you.

takushi dochira
タクシー…a taxi どちら …where

yokohama e ki
よこはまえき…Yokohama station

higashiguchi
ひがしぐち…East entrance

nishiguchi
にしぐち..West entrance

o machido u sama
おまちどうさま..thank you for the wait

reshi to o tsuri
レシート…receipt おつり…change

Let's practice

| とうきょうえき<br>なりたくうこう<br>ぎんざ | まで　おねがいします。 |
|---|---|

| ひがしぐち<br>とうきょう | ですか　それとも | にしぐち<br>おおさか | ですか。 |
|---|---|---|---|

| レシート<br>みず<br>コーヒー | を　おねがいします。 |
|---|---|

# resutoran de
# レストランで (At the Restaurant)

w e i toresu　　iras sha i mase
ウェイトレス：　いらっしゃいませ。

gochu u mo n wa　o kimari
ごちゅうもんは　おきまり

desuka
ですか。

sumisu　　ha i　ke　kise t to o mi t tsu
スミス：　はい。ケーキセットをみっつ

o nega i shimasu
おねがいします。

o nomimonowa
ウェイトレス：　おのみものは？

ko　hi　o　futatsuto
スミス：　コーヒーを　ふたつと

ko u cha o　hitotsu
こうちゃを　ひとつ

おねがいします。

kashikomarimashita
ウェイトレス：　はい、かしこまりました。

＊ ＊＊＊＊＊＊＊＊＊＊＊＊＊＊＊＊＊＊

o ka n　　u o
スミス：　おかんじょうを　おねがいします。

ウェイトレス：はい。

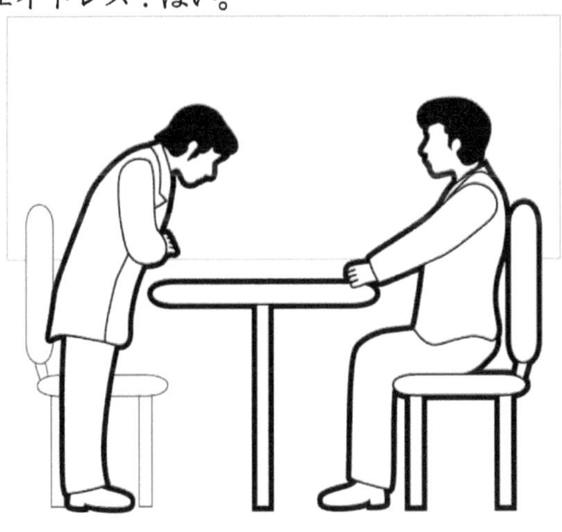

Waitress: Hello. Have you decided?
Smith: Yes, 3 cake-set, please.
Waitress: What would like for drink?
Smith: 2 coffees and 1 tea, please.
Waitress: Sure.

---

Smith: Please bring our bill.
Waitress: Sure.

gochuumon
ごちゅうもん（ちゅうもん）(your) order

okimari
おきまり…decided

ke kisetto
ケーキセット…a cake set

onomimono
おのみもの（のみもの）…a drink

okanjou wei toresu
おかんじょう…a bill ウェイトレス..a waitress

Let's practice

| ケーキセット<br>こうちゃ | を | 3つ<br>2つ | おねがいします。 |
|---|---|---|---|
| コーヒー<br>ハンバーグ | を | 2つ<br>3つ | と |
| こうちゃ<br>サラダ | を | 1つ<br>4つ | おねがいします。 |

depa　tode
## デパートで (At the Department Store)

te n i n　i ra s sha i mase
てんいん：いらっしゃいませ。

sumisu　kononiho n ni n gyo u wa　i kuradesu
スミス：　このにほんにんぎょうは　いくらです

ka
か。

korewa　desu
てんいん:　これは　１２0,０００です。

taka i desune
スミス：　たかいですね、、、

kochiranowa　i kagadesuka　sukoshi
てんいん:　こちらのは　いかがですか。すこし

chi i sa i desuga　e n
ちいさいですが、８０，０００えん

desu
です。

koremo　kire i desune　a rewa
スミス：　これも　きれいですね。あれは？

mo
てんいん：あれも　８0,０００えんです。

j a　o　kudasa i
スミス：　じゃ、あれを　ください。

kureji t toka　doga　tsuka e masuka
クレジットカードが　つかえますか。

ha i　i k katsudesuka　bu n katsuni
てんいん：はい。いっかつですか、ぶんかつに

nasa i masuka
なさいますか。

o nega i shimasu
スミス：　いっかつで　おねがいします。

Clerk: May I help you?
Smith: How much is this Japanese doll?
Clerk: This one is 120,000 yen.
Smith: Wow, it's expensive!
Clerk: How about this one? It's a little smaller but it is 80,000 yen.
Smith: This one is pretty, too. How about that one?
Clerk: That is also 80,000 yen.
Smith: Well, I'll take that one. Can I use credit card?
Clerk: Yes, would you like to pay in full or easy-payment system?
Smith: Pay in full, please.

nihonningyou
にほんにんぎょう….a Japanese doll

takai
たかい…expensive

yasui
やすい…inexpensive(cheap)

sukoshi
すこし… a little

chiisai
ちいさい…small

kirei
きれい…pretty

kurejittokado
クレジットカード…credit card

tsukaemasu tsukaeru
つかえます（つかえる）…can use

ikkatsu barai
いっかつ（ばらい）…pay in full

bunkatsu
ぶんかつ（ばらい）…payment by installments

haraimasu harau
はらいます（はらう）…pay

nasaru suru
なさる　　する….do

More verbs

kaemasu
かえます…can buy

kakemasu
かけます…can write

ikemasu
いけます…can go

hitori
ひとり…one person, alone

Let’s Practice

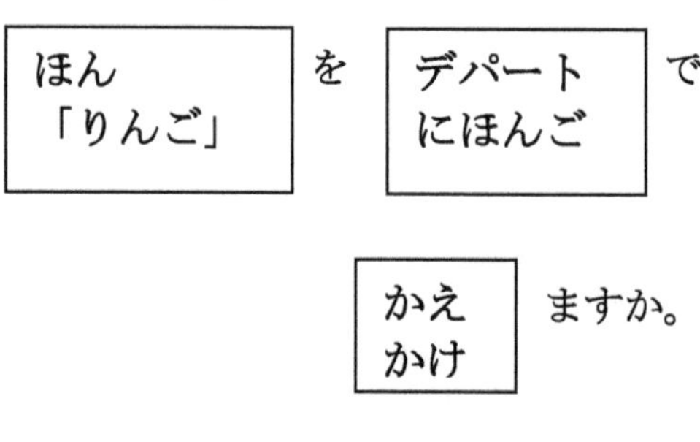

| ほん<br>「りんご」 | を | デパート<br>にほんご | で |
|---|---|---|---|

| かえ<br>かけ | ますか。 |
|---|---|

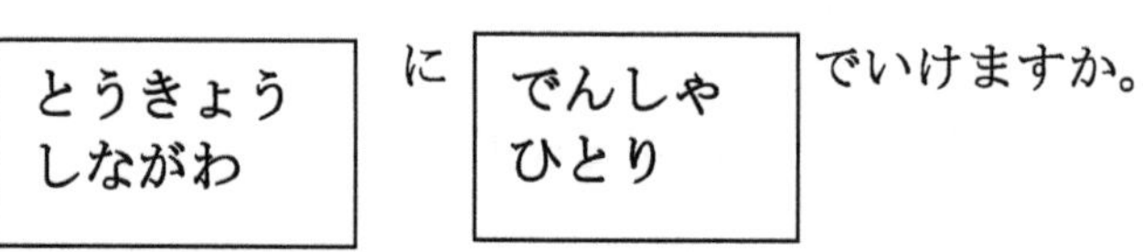

| とうきょう<br>しながわ | に | でんしゃ<br>ひとり | でいけますか。 |
|---|---|---|---|

## Useful Expressions

o hayo u goza i masu
おはようございます............... Good morning

ko n nichiwa
こんにちは...........................Good afternoon

ko n ba n wa
こんばんは........................... Good evening

sayo u nara
さようなら............................Good bye

shitsure i shimasu
し つれい します............Excuse me/Good bye

a rigato u goza i masu
ありがとう ございます......... .Thank you

sumimase n
すみません.................... Excuse me/Thank you

o medeto u goza i masu
おめでとう ございます............Congratulations

mo u i chido o nega i shimasu
もういちど おねがいします...Once more, please

## Family Members

| | Related to the speaker | Related to others |
|---|---|---|
| Family | kazoku<br>かぞく | gokazoku<br>ごかぞく |
| Parent | r yo u shi n<br>りょうしん | go r yo u shi n<br>ごりょうしん |
| Grandfather | sofu<br>そふ | o ji i sa n<br>おじいさん |
| Grandmother | sobo<br>そぼ | o ba a sa n<br>おばあさん |
| Father | chichi<br>ちち | o to u sa n<br>おとうさん |
| Mother | haha<br>はは | o ka a sa n<br>おかあさん |
| Husband | s hu ji n<br>しゅじん | go s hu ji n<br>ごしゅじん |
| Wife | tsuma／kana i<br>つま / かない | o kusa n<br>おくさん |
| Child | kodomo<br>こども | o kosa n ／kodomo<br>おこさん / こども<br>sa n<br>さん |
| Older brother | a ni<br>あに | o ni i sa n<br>おにいさん |
| Younger brother | o to u to<br>おとうと | o to u tosa n<br>おとうとさん |
| Daughter | musume<br>むすめ | musumesa n ／ o<br>むすめさん / お<br>j o u sa n<br>じょうさん |
| Older sister | a ne<br>あね | o ne e sa n<br>おねえさん |
| Younger sister | i mo u to<br>いもうと | i mo u tosa n<br>いもうとさん |
| Aunt | o ba<br>おば | o basa n<br>おばさん |
| Uncle | o ji<br>おじ | o jisa n<br>おじさん |

## The Seasons and Months

| | | | |
|---|---|---|---|
| haru<br>はる<br>Spring | natsu<br>なつ<br>Summer | a ki<br>あき<br>Fall/Autumn | fuyu<br>ふゆ<br>Winter |

| | | |
|---|---|---|
| i chigatsu<br>いちがつ<br>January | nigatsu<br>にがつ<br>February | sa n gatsu<br>さんがつ<br>March |
| shigatsu<br>しがつ<br>April | gogatsu<br>ごがつ<br>May | rokugatsu<br>ろくがつ<br>June |
| shichigatsu<br>しちがつ<br>July | hachigatsu<br>はちがつ<br>August | kugatsu<br>くがつ<br>September |
| j u u gatsu<br>じゅうがつ<br>October | j u u i chigatsu<br>じゅういちがつ<br>November | j u u nigatsu<br>じゅうにがつ<br>December |

## ひらがな（Hiragana)

| | | | | |
|---|---|---|---|---|
| あ ア | い イ | う ウ | え エ | お オ |
| a | i | u | e | o |
| か カ | き キ | く ク | け ケ | こ コ |
| ka | ki | ku | ke | ko |
| さ サ | し シ | す ス | せ セ | そ ソ |
| sa | shi | su | se | so |
| た タ | ち チ | つ ツ | て テ | と ト |
| ta | chi | tsu | te | to |
| な ナ | に ニ | ぬ ヌ | ね ネ | の ノ |
| na | ni | nu | ne | no |
| は ハ | ひ ヒ | ふ フ | へ ヘ | ほ ホ |
| ha | hi | fu | he | ho |
| ま マ | み ミ | む ム | め メ | も モ |
| ma | mi | mu | me | mo |
| や ヤ | | ゆ ユ | | よ ヨ |
| ya | | yu | | yo |
| ら ラ | り リ | る ル | れ レ | ろ ロ |
| ra | ri | ru | re | ro |
| わ ワ | | | | を ヲ |
| wa | | | | o |
| ん ン | | | | |
| n | | | | |

| | | |
|---|---|---|
| きゃ キャ | きゅ キュ | きょ キョ |
| kya | kyu | kyo |
| しゃ シャ | しゅ シュ | しょ ショ |
| sha | shu | sho |
| ちゃ チャ | ちゅ チュ | ちょ チョ |
| cha | chu | cho |
| にゃ ニャ | にゅ ニュ | にょ ニョ |
| nya | nyu | nyo |
| ひゃ ヒャ | ひゅ ヒュ | ひょ ヒョ |
| hya | hyu | hyo |
| みゃ ミャ | みゅ ミュ | みょ ミョ |
| mya | myu | myo |
| りゃ リャ | りゅ リュ | りょ リョ |
| rya | ryu | ryo |

## カタカナ（Katakana)

| が ガ | ぎ ギ | ぐ グ | げ ゲ | ご ゴ | ぎゃ ギャ | ぎゅ ギュ | ぎょ ギョ |
|---|---|---|---|---|---|---|---|
| ga | gi | gu | ge | go | gya | gyu | gyo |

| ざ ザ | じ ジ | ず ズ | ぜ ゼ | ぞ ゾ | じゃ ジャ | じゅ ジュ | じょ ジョ |
|---|---|---|---|---|---|---|---|
| za | ji | zu | ze | zo | ja | ju | jo |

| だ ダ | ぢ ヂ | づ ヅ | で デ | ど ド | ぢゃ ヂャ | ぢゅ ヂュ | ぢょ ヂョ |
|---|---|---|---|---|---|---|---|
| da | ji | zu | de | do | ja | ju | jo |

| ば バ | び ビ | ぶ ブ | べ べ | ぼ ボ | びゃ ビャ | びゅ ビュ | びょ ビョ |
|---|---|---|---|---|---|---|---|
| ba | bi | bu | be | bo | bya | byu | byo |
| ぱ パ | ぴ ピ | ぷ プ | ぺ ぺ | ぽ ポ | ぴゃ ピャ | ぴゅ ピュ | ぴょ ピョ |
| pa | pi | pu | pe | po | pya | pyu | pyo |

www.ingramcontent.com/pod-product-compliance
Ingram Content Group UK Ltd.
Pitfield, Milton Keynes, MK11 3LW, UK
UKHW041918190726
13854UKWH00003B/1314